ADDITION WORKBOOK

Kids will learn addition facts 0-18, find out how addition is related to subtraction, solve word problems, and learn addition strategies with this full-color workbook. Time tests are included so remember to reproduce the pages so young learners can practice over and over again against the clock.

Download the FREE Addition Songs:

1. The Island Of Learning
2. The Two-More-Than Strategy
3. I'm Jumpin' To The Beat Of The Music
4. What Do You Say?
5. The Fabulous Family Of Fives
6. I'm Hooked
7. Over And Over And Over Again
8. While We Exercise
9. It's Time To Review
10. I'm Talkin' About Doubles
11. Doubles Plus One

Visit www.twinsisters.com and enter the promo code

W1A5AD

Creative
TEACHING MATERIALS™

©℗2020 Twin Sisters IP, LLC. All Rights Reserved. Made In The U.S.A.

Written by: Kim Mitzo Thompson and Karen Mitzo Hilderbrand

Write how many.

100%

1.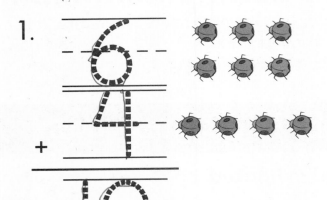

6
4
+
10   in all

2.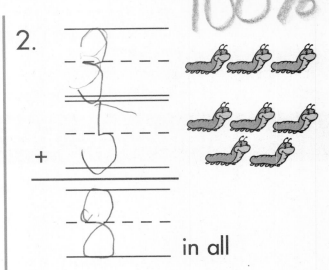

3
5
+
8   in all

3.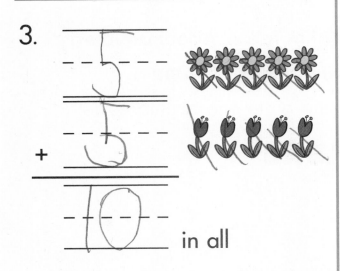

5
5
+
10   in all

4.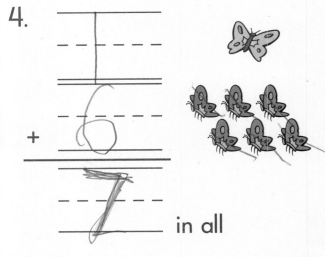

1
6
+
7   in all

5.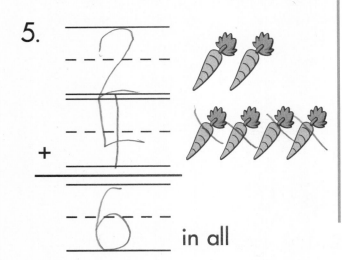

2
4
+
6   in all

6.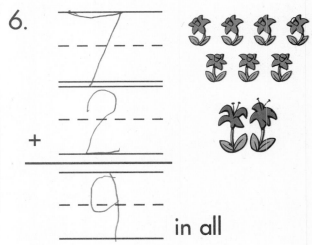

7
2
+
9   in all

Addition Number Sentences

Circle the correct number sentence.

1.

3 + 6

3 + 7 = 10

(3 + 6 = 9)

2.

(5 + 4 = 9)

5 + 5 = 10

3.

7 + 3 = 10

(8 + 2 = 10)

4.

6 + 3 = 9

(6 + 2 = 8)

5.

(0 + 7 = 7)

6 + 1 = 7

6.

3 + 6 = 9

(3 + 5 = 8)

Addition Facts to 10

Add to find the sums.

1.

$\begin{array}{r} 7 \\ +\ 3 \\ \hline \end{array}$	$\begin{array}{r} 5 \\ +\ 4 \\ \hline \end{array}$	$\begin{array}{r} 2 \\ +\ 2 \\ \hline \end{array}$	$\begin{array}{r} 2 \\ +\ 7 \\ \hline \end{array}$

2.

$\begin{array}{r} 0 \\ +\ 9 \\ \hline \end{array}$	$\begin{array}{r} 5 \\ +\ 2 \\ \hline \end{array}$	$\begin{array}{r} 3 \\ +\ 6 \\ \hline \end{array}$	$\begin{array}{r} 1 \\ +\ 2 \\ \hline \end{array}$

3.

$\begin{array}{r} 2 \\ +\ 8 \\ \hline \end{array}$	$\begin{array}{r} 3 \\ +\ 5 \\ \hline \end{array}$	$\begin{array}{r} 6 \\ +\ 1 \\ \hline \end{array}$	$\begin{array}{r} 2 \\ +\ 3 \\ \hline \end{array}$

Addition Facts to 10

Find the sums. Then use the code to color the picture.

10 = red   9 = blue   8 = green   7 = yellow   6 = orange

Addition Facts to 10

Add.

1.

$5 + 5 =$ _____ $3 + 3 =$ _____

2.

$8 + 1 =$ _____ $2 + 7 =$ _____

3.

$3 + 2 =$ _____ $3 + 0 =$ _____

4.

$6 + 3 =$ _____ $4 + 4 =$ _____

5.

$2 + 1 =$ _____ $6 + 4 =$ _____

6.

$5 + 2 =$ _____ $1 + 4 =$ _____

7.

$7 + 3 =$ _____ $6 + 0 =$ _____

Addition Word Problems

Read each problem. Write the answer.

1. Erin has 4 🐟.

   Mary has 2 🐟.

   How many 🐟 in all? _____

2. Bob has 2 🐸 s.

   David has 3 🐸 s.

   How many 🐸 s in all? _____

3. Susie picked 7 🌼 s.

   Jane picked 2 🌼 s.

   How many 🌼 s in all? _____

4. John has 5 🚗 s.

   Ed has 3 🚗 s.

   How many 🚗 s in all? _____

5. Jenny has 3 🧸 s.

   Joey has 1 🧸.

   How many 🧸 s in all? _____

Addition Word Problems

Read each problem. Write the answer.

1.
Rita sent 3 s.

Rob sent 6 s.

How many s in all?

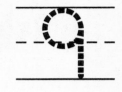

q

2.
Kate bought 6 s.

Ken bought 2 s.

How many s in all?

3.
Liz has 4 s.

Len has 3 s.

How many s in all?

4.
Zack has 2 s.

Matt has 2 s.

How many s in all?

Add.

1.

4	3	6	9	7
+ 6	+ 3	+ 2	+ 1	+ 0

2.

8	2	3	4	1
+ 1	+ 1	+ 6	+ 3	+ 4

3.

5	2	4	3	6
+ 5	+ 3	+ 4	+ 1	+ 2

4.

2	3	6	4	4
+ 8	+ 5	+ 0	+ 5	+ 1

Turnaround Addition Facts

The sum is the same.

Write the sums. Then match.

1.
$$5 + 4 = 9$$

$$2 + 6$$

2.
$$3 + 7$$

$$4 + 5 = 9$$

3.
$$6 + 2$$

$$7 + 0$$

4.
$$0 + 7$$

$$7 + 3$$

5.
$$3 + 2$$

$$2 + 3$$

6.
$$3 + 6$$

$$4 + 6$$

7.
$$5 + 2$$

$$6 + 3$$

8.
$$6 + 4$$

$$2 + 5$$

Number Line Addition

Write the missing *addend*. Finish drawing each problem on the number line.

0 1 2 3 4 5 6 7 8 9 10 11 12 13

$4 + 6 = 10$

0 1 2 3 4 5 6 7 8 9 10 11 12 13

$4 + \underline{} = 7$

0 1 2 3 4 5 6 7 8 9 10 11 12 13

$4 + \underline{} = 10$

0 1 2 3 4 5 6 7 8 9 10 11 12 13

$4 + \underline{} = 5$

0 1 2 3 4 5 6 7 8 9 10 11 12 13

$4 + \underline{} = 8$

0 1 2 3 4 5 6 7 8 9 10 11 12 13

$4 + \underline{} = 4$

0 1 2 3 4 5 6 7 8 9 10 11 12 13

$4 + \underline{} = 11$

5 Search

5+1=___   5+5=___   5+3=___   5+9=___   7+5=___

4+5=___   2+5=___   5+8=___   5+0=___   5+6=___

5	+	1	=	6	8	14	12
2	4	+	5	=	9	1	0
3	4	5	+	5	=	10	6
14	13	10	0	8	9	1	2
2	+	5	=	7	6	11	8
0	9	+	5	+	9	=	14
9	6	3	7	5	1	6	6
14	5	=	13	=	8	+	5
11	1	8	2	12	3	5	4

12

Addition Practice: +5

5
+ ◯
10

7
+ 5
◯

◯
+ 5
7

◯
+ 4
9

5
+ ◯
6

5
+ ◯
11

◯
+ 5
14

5
+ ◯
13

5
+ ◯
7

◯
+ 5
6

5
+ ◯
12

4
+ ◯
9

6
+ 5
◯

5
+ ◯
10

◯
+ 3
8

3
+ ◯
8

5
+ ◯
9

6
+ ◯
11

2
+ ◯
7

5
+ ◯
6

8 Search

Add the *addends* and write the *sum*. Find and circle each fact and write a + or = sign in the correct place.

8+1=___   8+5=___   1+8=___   3+8=___

8+9=___   8+3=___   9+8=___   2+8=___

8+7=___   8+2=___   7+8=___   0+8=___

8+6=___   8+0=___   6+8=___

8+5=___   8+8=___   5+8=___

9	8	0	8	11	1	8 + 1 = 9	0
5	2	7	8	6	14	13	7	6	7
1	10	9	16	3	9	8	17	12	8
8	6	8	14	1	8	12	17	13	15
4	5	2	3	0	1	13	6	8	14
12	8	7	15	11	5	0	3	5	7
2	3	5	9	8	5	13	0	1	14
17	11	13	1	6	0	16	8	9	17
5	9	2	8	10	5	3	8	11	9

14

Addition: Sets

Count. Write how many.

1.

             9   +   9   =   **in all**
18

2.

      _ _ _ _   +   _ _ _ _   =   **in all**
_ _ _ _

3.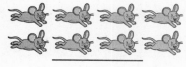

      _ _ _ _   +   _ _ _ _   =   **in all**
_ _ _ _

4.

      _ _ _ _ _   +   _ _ _ _   =   **in all**
_ _ _ _

5.

      _ _ _ _ _   +   _ _ _ _   =   **in all**
_ _ _ _

Addition: Sets

Write how many.

1.
$$9$$
$$+\ 8$$
_____
17
_ _ _ _ _
_____ in all

2.
$$8$$
$$+\ 7$$
_____
_ _ _ _ _
_____ in all

3.
$$8$$
$$+\ 9$$
_____
_ _ _ _ _
_____ in all

4.
$$9$$
$$+\ 7$$
_____
_ _ _ _ _
_____ in all

5.
$$6$$
$$+\ 9$$
_____
_ _ _ _ _
_____ in all

6.
$$6$$
$$+\ 7$$
_____
_ _ _ _ _
_____ in all

7.
$$7$$
$$+\ 7$$
_____
_ _ _ _ _
_____ in all

Addition Facts to 18

Add to find the sums.

1.

   9   +   9   = $\underline{18}$

2.   _____

   9 + 8 = _____   9 + 7 = _____

3.   _____   _____   _____

   3 + 8 = _____   9 + 3 = _____   8 + 5 = _____

4.   _____   _____   _____

   8 + 4 = _____   7 + 7 = _____   9 + 6 = _____

5.   _____   _____   _____

   8 + 8 = _____   9 + 2 = _____   5 + 7 = _____

6.   _____   _____   _____

   8 + 6 = _____   4 + 7 = _____   6 + 6 = _____

$$\begin{array}{r} 10 \\ +\ 8 \\ \hline 18 \end{array}$$

Add to find the sums.

1.

$$\begin{array}{r} 9 \\ +\ 8 \\ \hline \end{array}$$
$$\begin{array}{r} 9 \\ +\ 2 \\ \hline \end{array}$$
$$\begin{array}{r} 9 \\ +\ 9 \\ \hline \end{array}$$
$$\begin{array}{r} 6 \\ +\ 8 \\ \hline \end{array}$$
$$\begin{array}{r} 7 \\ +\ 5 \\ \hline \end{array}$$

2.

$$\begin{array}{r} 6 \\ +\ 9 \\ \hline \end{array}$$
$$\begin{array}{r} 7 \\ +\ 6 \\ \hline \end{array}$$
$$\begin{array}{r} 9 \\ +\ 5 \\ \hline \end{array}$$
$$\begin{array}{r} 8 \\ +\ 8 \\ \hline \end{array}$$
$$\begin{array}{r} 6 \\ +\ 6 \\ \hline \end{array}$$

3.

$$\begin{array}{r} 3 \\ +\ 8 \\ \hline \end{array}$$
$$\begin{array}{r} 5 \\ +\ 8 \\ \hline \end{array}$$
$$\begin{array}{r} 7 \\ +\ 4 \\ \hline \end{array}$$
$$\begin{array}{r} 4 \\ +\ 8 \\ \hline \end{array}$$
$$\begin{array}{r} 7 \\ +\ 7 \\ \hline \end{array}$$

Now I'm Talkin' About Doubles Strategy

$1+1=$ ____

$4+4=$ ____

$7+7=$ ____

$2+2=$ ____

$5+5=$ ____

$8+8=$ ____

$3+3=$ ____

$6+6=$ ____

$9+9=$ ____

$$\begin{array}{r} 7 \\ +7 \\ \hline \end{array}$$

$$\begin{array}{r} 1 \\ +1 \\ \hline \end{array}$$

$$\begin{array}{r} 5 \\ +5 \\ \hline \end{array}$$

$$\begin{array}{r} 3 \\ +3 \\ \hline \end{array}$$

$$\begin{array}{r} 2 \\ +2 \\ \hline \end{array}$$

$$\begin{array}{r} 9 \\ +9 \\ \hline \end{array}$$

$$\begin{array}{r} 8 \\ +8 \\ \hline \end{array}$$

$$\begin{array}{r} 6 \\ +6 \\ \hline \end{array}$$

$$\begin{array}{r} 4 \\ +4 \\ \hline \end{array}$$

Practice your doubles by saying, "One doubled is Two." See how quickly you can say the doubles one through nine this way! Have someone time you!

Study the sums of the doubles above. What do all the doubles have in common? Turn this page upside down to learn the answer.

Answer: All double facts are even numbers—always!

Addition Practice

$$\begin{array}{r} 2 \\ + 7 \\ \hline 9 \end{array}$$

○ 8
● 9
○ 10

Solve. Then fill in the circle next to the correct answer.

1.
$$\begin{array}{r} 7 \\ + 4 \\ \hline \end{array}$$
○ 10
○ 13
○ 11

2.
$$\begin{array}{r} 4 \\ + 5 \\ \hline \end{array}$$
○ 8
○ 9
○ 10

3.
$$\begin{array}{r} 5 \\ + 3 \\ \hline \end{array}$$
○ 6
○ 7
○ 8

4.
$$\begin{array}{r} 8 \\ + 7 \\ \hline \end{array}$$
○ 14
○ 15
○ 12

5.
$$\begin{array}{r} 4 \\ + 2 \\ \hline \end{array}$$
○ 6
○ 5
○ 4

6.
$$\begin{array}{r} 2 \\ + 9 \\ \hline \end{array}$$
○ 12
○ 13
○ 11

7.
$$\begin{array}{r} 3 \\ + 7 \\ \hline \end{array}$$
○ 10
○ 11
○ 12

8.
$$\begin{array}{r} 8 \\ + 3 \\ \hline \end{array}$$
○ 11
○ 13
○ 10

Addition Practice

$$7 + 4 = 11$$

Write the missing number.

1.

6		8	
+	+ 9	+	+ 9
14	12	13	17

2.

		9	9
+ 8	+ 6	+	+
16	15	18	13

3.

3		5	
+	+ 7	+	+ 7
11	13	15	14

Addition Practice

$8 + 3 = 11$

○ 10
● 11
○ 12

Solve. Then fill in the circle next to the correct answer.

1.

$6 + 6 = \rule{2cm}{0.4pt}$

○ 11
○ 12
○ 15

2.

$2 + 9 = \rule{2cm}{0.4pt}$

○ 9
○ 10
○ 11

3.

$5 + 6 = \rule{2cm}{0.4pt}$

○ 11
○ 12
○ 13

4.

$7 + 7 = \rule{2cm}{0.4pt}$

○ 14
○ 19
○ 16

5.

$9 + 9 = \rule{2cm}{0.4pt}$

○ 17
○ 20
○ 18

6.

$8 + 6 = \rule{2cm}{0.4pt}$

○ 12
○ 13
○ 14

7.

$7 + 4 = \rule{2cm}{0.4pt}$

○ 10
○ 11
○ 12

8.

$8 + 8 = \rule{2cm}{0.4pt}$

○ 15
○ 16
○ 19

Addition Word Problems

Read each problem. Write the answer.

1.

Kim has 5 s.

She got 6 more s.

How many s does she have now?

$$\begin{array}{r} 5 \\ + 6 \\ \hline \end{array}$$

- - - - -

_____

2.

Rick found 8 s.

Pam found 7 s.

How many s did they find in all?

$$\begin{array}{r} 8 \\ + 7 \\ \hline \end{array}$$

- - - - -

_____

3.

Matt has 6 s.

Rob has 9 s.

How many s do they have in all?

$$\begin{array}{r} 6 \\ + 9 \\ \hline \end{array}$$

- - - - -

_____

4.

Pat has 7 s.

Her mother gave her 4 more.

How many s does she have now?

$$\begin{array}{r} 7 \\ + 4 \\ \hline \end{array}$$

- - - - -

_____

Addition Word Problems

Read each problem. Write the answer.

1.

Ryan saw 7 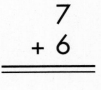s.

Then he saw 6 more s.

How many s did he see in all?

$$\begin{array}{r} 7 \\ + 6 \\ \hline \end{array}$$

- - - - -
_____

2.

Nick collected 8 s.

He found 3 more s.

How many s did he have in all?

$$\begin{array}{r} 8 \\ + 3 \\ \hline \end{array}$$

- - - - -
_____

3.

Ashley planted 9 s.

Frank planted 4 s.

How many s were planted in all?

$$\begin{array}{r} 9 \\ + 4 \\ \hline \end{array}$$

- - - - -
_____

4.

Kyle has 9 s.

His dad gave him 8 more s.

How many s does he have now?

$$\begin{array}{r} 9 \\ + 8 \\ \hline \end{array}$$

- - - - -
_____

Secret Code

Add the *addends*. Match the letter and the *sum* in the code to solve the riddle.

Code

T	O	S	I	E	U	H	!	D
10	11	12	13	14	15	16	17	18

What side of the chicken do feathers grow on?

1 +9	9 +7	5 +9

2 +9	6 +9	1 +9	9 +3	4 +9	9 +9	9 +5	8 +9

25

Target Practice

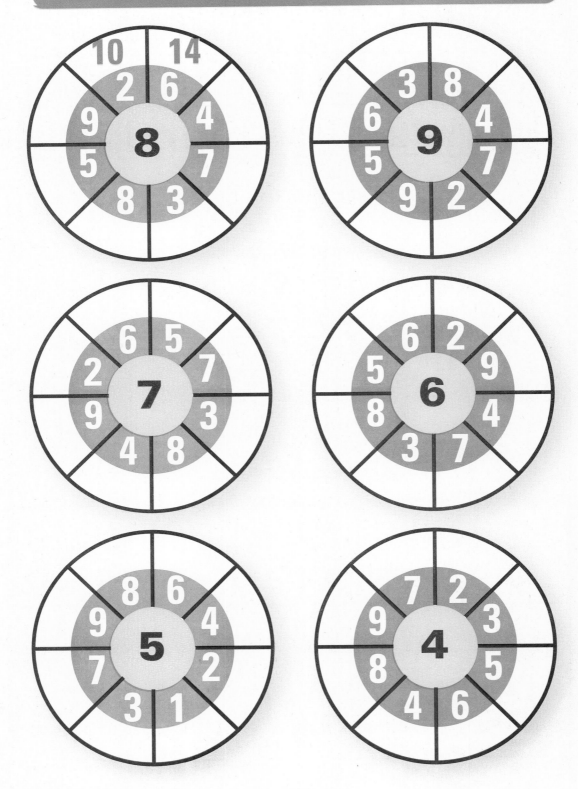

Addition Review

3+4=
- 5
- 6
- 7

2+9=
- 9
- 10
- 11

1+5=
- 6
- 4
- 0

5+6=
- 11
- 12
- 13

4+9=
- 12
- 13
- 14

8+6=
- 14
- 11
- 12

0+6=
- 0
- 6
- 1

6+6=
- 12
- 13
- 14

3+8=
- 9
- 10
- 11

7+4=
- 10
- 11
- 12

9+9=
- 17
- 18
- 19

8+7=
- 15
- 16
- 17

9+4=
- 13
- 14
- 15

4+8=
- 11
- 12
- 13

7+5=
- 10
- 11
- 12

7+1=
- 6
- 7
- 8

8+8=
- 14
- 15
- 16

4+7=
- 3
- 11
- 10

27

3 + 5	7 + 7	1 + 9	3 + 8	3 + 6
5 + 7	6 + 9	9 + 5	9 + 2	6 + 7
4 + 6	0 + 3	3 + 9	2 + 7	3 + 1
2 + 2	3 + 4	9 + 7	1 + 4	5 + 5
0 + 1	3 + 8	4 + 3	2 + 0	9 + 4

$$8 + 1 \qquad 7 + 8 \qquad 6 + 6 \qquad 6 + 2 \qquad 8 + 3$$

$$7 + 4 \qquad 6 + 8 \qquad 8 + 9 \qquad 3 + 4 \qquad 2 + 3$$

$$5 + 6 \qquad 4 + 2 \qquad 6 + 4 \qquad 9 + 3 \qquad 8 + 8$$

$$7 + 6 \qquad 3 + 5 \qquad 9 + 9 \qquad 5 + 6 \qquad 7 + 5$$

$$9 + 7 \qquad 5 + 2 \qquad 3 + 4 \qquad 8 + 2 \qquad 9 + 7$$

0 + 9	4 + 6	2 + 6	3 + 7	4 + 5
5 + 8	6 + 4	7 + 7	0 + 0	9 + 5
2 + 6	9 + 3	7 + 4	2 + 1	1 + 0
9 + 7	1 + 5	9 + 1	7 + 8	5 + 2
1 + 1	5 + 6	9 + 8	8 + 4	9 + 6

$\begin{array}{r} 1 \\ + 5 \\ \hline \end{array}$	$\begin{array}{r} 4 \\ + 7 \\ \hline \end{array}$	$\begin{array}{r} 5 \\ + 6 \\ \hline \end{array}$	$\begin{array}{r} 6 \\ + 8 \\ \hline \end{array}$	$\begin{array}{r} 3 \\ + 6 \\ \hline \end{array}$
$\begin{array}{r} 7 \\ + 7 \\ \hline \end{array}$	$\begin{array}{r} 2 \\ + 2 \\ \hline \end{array}$	$\begin{array}{r} 5 \\ + 5 \\ \hline \end{array}$	$\begin{array}{r} 9 \\ + 8 \\ \hline \end{array}$	$\begin{array}{r} 8 \\ + 7 \\ \hline \end{array}$
$\begin{array}{r} 7 \\ + 6 \\ \hline \end{array}$	$\begin{array}{r} 5 \\ + 0 \\ \hline \end{array}$	$\begin{array}{r} 1 \\ + 4 \\ \hline \end{array}$	$\begin{array}{r} 1 \\ + 7 \\ \hline \end{array}$	$\begin{array}{r} 3 \\ + 8 \\ \hline \end{array}$
$\begin{array}{r} 5 \\ + 6 \\ \hline \end{array}$	$\begin{array}{r} 3 \\ + 5 \\ \hline \end{array}$	$\begin{array}{r} 8 \\ + 7 \\ \hline \end{array}$	$\begin{array}{r} 7 \\ + 6 \\ \hline \end{array}$	$\begin{array}{r} 9 \\ + 5 \\ \hline \end{array}$
$\begin{array}{r} 7 \\ + 5 \\ \hline \end{array}$	$\begin{array}{r} 6 \\ + 7 \\ \hline \end{array}$	$\begin{array}{r} 8 \\ + 6 \\ \hline \end{array}$	$\begin{array}{r} 3 \\ + 9 \\ \hline \end{array}$	$\begin{array}{r} 9 \\ + 8 \\ \hline \end{array}$
$\begin{array}{r} 5 \\ + 7 \\ \hline \end{array}$	$\begin{array}{r} 4 \\ + 5 \\ \hline \end{array}$	$\begin{array}{r} 2 \\ + 6 \\ \hline \end{array}$	$\begin{array}{r} 1 \\ + 8 \\ \hline \end{array}$	$\begin{array}{r} 6 \\ + 9 \\ \hline \end{array}$
$\begin{array}{r} 1 \\ + 8 \\ \hline \end{array}$	$\begin{array}{r} 4 \\ + 5 \\ \hline \end{array}$	$\begin{array}{r} 7 \\ + 7 \\ \hline \end{array}$	$\begin{array}{r} 3 \\ + 8 \\ \hline \end{array}$	$\begin{array}{r} 2 \\ + 7 \\ \hline \end{array}$
$\begin{array}{r} 3 \\ + 6 \\ \hline \end{array}$	$\begin{array}{r} 9 \\ + 9 \\ \hline \end{array}$	$\begin{array}{r} 3 \\ + 1 \\ \hline \end{array}$	$\begin{array}{r} 5 \\ + 5 \\ \hline \end{array}$	$\begin{array}{r} 6 \\ + 7 \\ \hline \end{array}$
$\begin{array}{r} 4 \\ + 2 \\ \hline \end{array}$	$\begin{array}{r} 7 \\ + 7 \\ \hline \end{array}$	$\begin{array}{r} 5 \\ + 2 \\ \hline \end{array}$	$\begin{array}{r} 6 \\ + 6 \\ \hline \end{array}$	$\begin{array}{r} 8 \\ + 6 \\ \hline \end{array}$
$\begin{array}{r} 7 \\ + 9 \\ \hline \end{array}$	$\begin{array}{r} 6 \\ + 4 \\ \hline \end{array}$	$\begin{array}{r} 6 \\ + 8 \\ \hline \end{array}$	$\begin{array}{r} 2 \\ + 8 \\ \hline \end{array}$	$\begin{array}{r} 4 \\ + 7 \\ \hline \end{array}$

$4 + 9$	$0 + 1$	$7 + 7$	$4 + 8$	$5 + 9$
$9 + 9$	$3 + 5$	$8 + 9$	$6 + 6$	$9 + 2$
$1 + 9$	$3 + 7$	$3 + 9$	$8 + 5$	$1 + 3$
$7 + 6$	$3 + 5$	$6 + 5$	$2 + 0$	$8 + 9$
$2 + 8$	$4 + 8$	$3 + 7$	$8 + 8$	$6 + 7$
$3 + 5$	$9 + 9$	$5 + 6$	$7 + 5$	$9 + 7$
$3 + 2$	$4 + 6$	$9 + 2$	$6 + 4$	$8 + 2$
$4 + 7$	$2 + 6$	$5 + 1$	$9 + 3$	$7 + 2$
$1 + 2$	$4 + 3$	$5 + 2$	$6 + 4$	$3 + 2$
$7 + 2$	$6 + 3$	$5 + 1$	$9 + 1$	$8 + 2$